This book is presented to:

_____

_____

From:

_____

_____

On:

_____
(Date)

Un-Stuckness:
Keys to Deliverance through Prayer Jesus' Way

By Jamillah Cupe

Copyright © 2016 Jamillah Cupe

Unless otherwise noted, all scriptures are from the King James Version of the Holy Bible.

A Publication of Un-Stuckness Ministries, LLC
PO Box 22472
Newark, NJ 07101

For more information on Jamillah Cupe visit
www.unstuckness.com

PRINTED IN THE UNITED STATES OF AMERICA

All rights reserved. No part of this book may be reproduced or transmitted in any form or by any means, electronically or mechanically, including photocopying, recording, and/or by information storage or retrieval systems without the written permission from the publisher, except in the case of brief quotations. For information address Un-Stuckness Ministries Rights Department, P.O. Box 22472, Newark, NJ 07101.

ISBN -10:0692951415
ISBN-13: 978-0692951415

ATTENTION, CORPORATIONS, UNIVERSITIES, COLLEGES, MINISTRIES AND PROFESSIONAL ORGANIZATIONS: Quantity discounts are available on bulk purchases of this book for educational and gift purposes. For more information, please contact Un-Stuckness Ministries Special Sales, P.O. Box 22472, Newark NJ, 07101.

Dedication

To my children Mirandah, Anaiah and Josiah. Those I have mentored and labored with in prayer. And others who are simply seeking to learn how to pray and receive individual deliverance, especially from un-forgiveness.

This book is transformational! You will learn how to pray quickly, effectively and receive deliverance. Your prayer life and walk with God will never be the same! *Keys To Deliverance* is anointed to open eyes, heal, deliver and set free. So be set free and move forward embracing God's will and purpose— this is what Jesus Christ died and rose on the third day for!

Table of Contents

Dedication	v
Acknowledgment	xi
Introduction	xiii
Chapter 1: What is Deliverance?	41
Chapter 2: Good Advice	65
Chapter 3: The Keys to Deliverance	85
Chapter 4: Dissecting the Lord's Prayer	107
Chapter 5: How to Pray Jesus' Way	113
Chapter 6: Conclusion	135
Becoming A Child of God	144

Acknowledgment

I give thanks the our Heavenly Father, His resurrected son Jesus Christ and the Holy Spirit, who protects, heals, delivers, restores and redeems. The provider of knowledge, wisdom, understanding, power and solutions. My present help! The giver of life—

Abba father.

Introduction
WHAT TO EXPECT FROM THIS BOOK

Un-Stuckness

This book is Vol. 2 to *Un-Stuckness: Breaking Generational Chains and Strongholds Through Prayer*. After reading this book you will surely know how to pray effectively, break barriers and release hurtful experiences. **Un-Stuckness: Keys to Deliverance** place special emphases on deliverance, what deliverance is, the importance of it and how to maintain it once it is received. It also includes important principles that one should consider or apply in conjunction with embracing a lifestyle of prayer and seeking God.

Furthermore, significantly it demonstrates how praying the Lord's Prayer daily can be an effective way to pray and receive deliverance in all areas that have kept you stuck mentally, emotionally, spiritually, socially and financially. It is a guide that Jesus Christ provided as an aid for the sons and daughters of God to be filtered of contaminates, gain strengthen and become restored as long as it is prayed sincerely.

Jesus, while on earth, healed the sick, delivered those were bound by demonic influences,

Keys to Deliverance through Prayer
Jesus' Way

performed many miracles and commanded His disciples to do the same (Matthew 19:8; Matthew 23-24). He came for the lost and oppressed, knowing that only the sick and afflicted need a physician (Matthew 9:12; Luke 19:10).

One way sickness and afflictions impact many individuals is when they are unable to cope with traumatic, shocking, depressing and shameful experiences or mistakes. Failure to resolve such of issues can make it a struggle to forgive and move forward in life.

Negative emotions from unresolved bad experiences and offenses, often caused by people who were closely related or connected to them, create toxins. Emotional toxins flow through the mind, body, spirit and soul infecting the mental, physical, spiritual and emotional body with various sicknesses.

People may blame their experience on God instead of the devil and say "Why did God allow this terrible thing to happen?" or "Why did not God….?" They may feel angry with God and may

Un-Stuckness

not want to serve or seek Him for this reason alone. They may not know that it is likely that the experience was against God's plans.

In addition, they fail to realize that just as God has plans for us, which are not of harm but of good, to prosper and guide us into a bright future, Satan has plans to counteract God's plans, by plotting against us. He sets up opportunities to attack and bring us harm (Jeremiah 29:11; John 10:10).

Satan's goal is to still, kill and destroy our mental and spiritual peace and future. He hopes to hinder our destiny and place a cap on our ability to progress successfully and healthy; so that we can never reach the level of success God desire. With this in mind, it is for this reason, when Satan plot his aim to strike us with devastating experiences. Hoping we will lose our mind, hope, dreams and become stagnated. As you may know, there are some experiences that can be very hard to overcome.

Keys to Deliverance through Prayer Jesus' Way

But God is able to step in and reverse the effects of every dramatic situation that Satan thought would destroy your mind, spirit, and will to succeded in the future. The power of God can change your life! God is able to help and heal you in any area in which you give Him permission and access! He specializes in succeeding where man has failed.

People who read *Un-Stuckness: Keys to Deliverance through Prayer Jesus' Way,* believe they do not know how to pray and want to learn how to pray more effectively can expect to find this book to be beneficial in teaching these skills. Additionally, people who are battling tough issues and want to take responsibility for participating in their own deliverance and salvation will find keys in this book that would bring relief, positive changes and desired positive outcomes.

For God is the creator of man, earth and beyond, what can really be too hard for Him to fix? He desires for his children to keep Him first in everything. To worship daily to seek His face and

Un-Stuckness

to cry out to Him concerning every distressful situation (Psalm 34:17). When they do this sincerely, He shows up, answers and delivers.

Do you know that it is essential to have an approach with the right mind, heart and intentions, especially when seeking an encounter from God? Because God knows the heart of man, a sincere and honest approach will help reveal and open the door to who God is and provide you with guidance concerning the right path.

God said seek and you will find, knock and the door will open (Matthew 7:7-12; Luke 11:9). This book will show you how to knock, seek and find. However, with the right mindset and heart you will obtain answers speedily. Just remember to seek ye first the kingdom of God and His righteousness and everything else will follow.

The mental attitude you adopt towards prayer when seeking the Lord and also in your day-to-day life experiences, challenges, goals and treatment of others will determine your success, accomplishments, failures or setbacks. **Mental attitude is everything!**

Do you know, that the word of God also makes clear that the path to transformation is achieved through the practice of renewing your mind (Romans 12:2)? Therefore, you must be willing to allow the power of God to filter your mind from all negative thinking that will block your success and prosperity.

The word of God teaches us that as a man thinks in his heart so is he (Proverbs 23:7). So, for this reason, if you think you will prosper, you will prosper, if you think you will fail, you will not obtain success. Simultaneously, if you think happy thoughts, you will feel, act and experience happiness. The state of your mind determines your quality of life.

Similarly, if you entertain angry thoughts, you will act and feel angry. Proverbs 17: 22 states that "A merry heart doeth good like a medicine: but a broken spirit drieth the bones." Let your mind be

Un-Stuckness

transformed by the words of God, good memories, positive thoughts and encouraging things.

Becoming fueled with the strong mental determination that your life must change for the better is the first step necessary to mandate an end to old cycles and negative thought patterns that create stagnation in your ability to move forward into God's purpose.

It is important to grant God permission to drain all pollution from your mind, memories and every area of your life that has kept you from advancing productively. If you want to move forward, God is more than able to heal, restore, reprogram and regulate your mind and thinking habits. If you lay all that has been too much to carry at His feet, He will carry the weight for you.

It would be very difficult to achieve a better outlook and a new chapter in your life while holding onto negative thoughts (Isaiah 43:18). It would be a struggle to move forward and eliminate unproductive cycles from repeating themselves while holding onto pain, shame and regrets. You need a new transformed mind in order to push pass old limits.

God makes all things new and daily loads His children with benefits, so if you want a changed and improved life, there is no reason why it cannot happen (Isaiah 43:19; Psalm 68:19). When you become born again in Jesus Christ, you become a new creation; all old things pass away and God makes you and all things new (2 Corinthians 5:17). God can grant you a new mind, new ways, new characters and a new lifestyle.

Life is full of constant changes, and it is okay for you to decide to make a new change that will ultimately become essential in transforming your life and future for the better (Ecclesiastes 3: 1-80). What you obtain in life is according to your beliefs. It's normal to initially feel insecure walking into unfamiliar steps. However, this path is necessary for you to discover how to walk by faith and not by sight. You'll learn to trust God more than your own rationale.

Un-Stuckness

Unfortunately, you will only experience life as a constant circle, (repeating various experiences) if you DO NOT push pass what feels uncomfortable and unfamiliar. It takes both being brave enough to surrender what you think you know and trusting in God's ability to heal and transform your life by faith.

Everything connected to your head must be transformed by the experience of God. By renewing your mind, speaking what you want to see, using the right words, writing your vison and goals, and praying, your life can change. But you must BELIEVE! You must have FAITH! You must TRY!

Any limits you allow to remain in your thinking process concerning what you believe you can achieve or doubting the possibility that old habits can break, should be deleted and removed for good. For example, the "I can't," and all other excuses should be eliminated. Otherwise, it will be impossible for you to receive that which you do not believe or have faith to believe. Your total approach and mindset must be one that does not place boundaries on the capabilities and power of God to heal, transform and change your life.

In order to get un-stuck, delivered, healed and changed, there must be firm willpower and internal sincerity that you are willing to surrender being right in your own mind, ways, understanding. You must ultimately embrace the will and way of God.

With the right heart and intent, those that seek God will find Him and those that desire a change will receive the transformation of their heart's desire. God looks at the heart and is not moved by people who only praise Him with their mouth but those that have a heart sincerely craving closeness with Him (Matthew 15:8, Isaiah 29:13).

As you participate in the reading of this book and seek your deliverance from situations that are gripping your life, it would be very helpful for you to embrace daily scriptures and prayers that will strengthen your belief. The word of God is able to clean, reinforce a sound mind and filter out doubt and fear (John 15:3).

Un-Stuckness

Looking up scriptures that support the subject in which you are seeking a breakthrough would help you gain mental and spiritual strength. Put the scripture on index cards or create a journal. Then review them every day and night and meditate on them throughout the day. It is a great practice to think on the things that are good and not of evil.

The enemy only needs a small entrance into your mind and thoughts to bring chaos that will spread into your entire life. God keeps those in perfect peace whose mind stays on Him. When you make meditating on the word of God a lifestyle, the peace of God will surround you.

"Blessed is the man that walketh not in the counsel of the ungodly, nor standeth in the way of sinners, nor sitteth in the seat of the scornful. But his delight is in the law of the Lord; and in his law doth he meditate day and night. And he shall be like a tree planted by the rivers of water, that bringeth forth his fruit in his season; his leaf also shall not wither; and whatsoever he doeth shall prosper (Psalm 1:1-3).*"*

Keys to Deliverance through Prayer Jesus' Way

Daily meditating on the word and promises of God is a practice that would not be in vain when you take the time to do so. It can be compared to any relationship; you reap the rewards from the quality time you put in. Spending time in the word of God would allow you to grow strong and become unmovable in the Lord.

Following are a few examples of ways to meditate on scriptures. Continue praying and utilizing them until you receive your victory.

[Scripture Meditation/Prayer Examples]

1. **Philippians 4:13 I can do all things through Christ which strengtheneth me.** (When you believe in this scripture NOTHING can block, stop, limit or prevent your victory! (Every mountain and hill shall be made low. The word of God is strong and powerful enough to crush every mountain into small pieces.) I can do all things through Jesus Christ who strengthens me. I will not limit my potential

and I will not limit the power of God to change, flow, move and operate in my life. I can do all things through Jesus Christ. I can receive my deliverance, healing, ability to move forward, be fruitful and prosper in all areas of my life. I will succeed and be successful. I can set goals and achieve them all. I will reach high for I am the head and not the tail. Things that held me back yesterday will no longer overpower my life today, in the name of Jesus Christ.

2. **2 Corinthians 5:17 Therefore if any man be in Christ, he is a new creature: old things are passed away; behold, all things are become new.** I am made new in Christ Jesus. My past, failures, hurtful experiences, insecurities, pain, mistakes, rejections, confusion, fears, limitations, and hardships have passed away and died with Christ. I decree and declare that I am now risen with Christ. I am reborn, made new,

whole and complete in Christ Jesus. My mind is new. I now have the mind of Christ. I have a renewed mind, a sound mind and my heart is new and all experiences are new. In the name of Jesus, I have a new life and I have it abundantly. Nothing will stop my ability to prosper and move forward, in Jesus' Name.

3. **Galatians 6:9 And let us not be weary in well doing: for in due season we shall reap, if we faint not.** (Sometimes when you try to do the right things and the enemy comes it's like a flood, it's a difficult season. Your eyes and mind must be fixed, focused and undistracted on the word of God regardless of what situations and challenges come before you; stay anchored.) In the name of Jesus Christ, I will not become weary in well doing. I will not faint nor will I give up, no matter how great the challenge or difficulty before me. I will walk in faith

and practice to not be moved by sight, images, bad reports and memories. I will walk in hope and soak my mind in the word of God, meditate day and night and pray in my heart without ceasing. I will continue to move forward and cut every cord that wants to keep me stuck. I will reap all the blessings and benefits of serving the Lord and continuously walk in victory.

4. **Psalm 23 He restoreth my soul: he leadeth me in the paths of righteousness for his name's sake.** Father God, I pray to be restored. Restore me where I have been wounded. Restore me in every area I have been injured. I seek to be restored and made whole. For thy name sake O, God restore me. Restore my mind, body, spirit, soul, heart and character completely. Please guide and lead me on a path of righteousness as I embrace a new positive change for my life. Lead me in the

right direction, the right helpers, ministry, relationships, church and career. Restore my life completely O God, for you are my hope and only refuge, in Jesus' name I pray.

5. **Psalm 23:4 Yea, though I walk through the valley of the shadow of death, I will fear no evil: for thou art with me; thy rod and thy staff they comfort me.** Father, walk with me, guide my eyes, hands and feet as I embrace a new chapter in my life. Order my steps and guide my ways. Let your grace be upon me, to remain anchored in you despite any challenges or hardships that may arise. Let me fear no evil, bad report or challenge and may your presence comfort, protect and be my shield and buckler forever, in Jesus' name.

6. **Jeremiah 29:11 For I know the thoughts that I think toward you, saith the Lord, thoughts of peace, and not of evil, to**

give you an expected end. O Lord, let me receive the expected end that you desire for my life. Grant me the grace to walk in the highest level of success that I can achieve in life, health, home, family, children, career and ministry. Cancel every situation that will disrupt my peace today in Jesus' name. Cancel every evil situation and plot to bring hardship in my life, family, children, health and finances. Father let your expected end for my life overrule every evil plan of the enemy and let your peace overshadow me as a garment in Jesus' name. I decree and declare that I will reach and fulfill the expected end you have for my life in Jesus' name.

7. **2 Timothy 1:7 For God hath not given us the spirit of fear; but of power, and of love, and of a sound mind.** Father, in the name of Jesus I come to you asking that you cover me with the blood of Jesus

Christ and uproot every implantation of fear that was planted in my life from my youth and until presently this day. I refuse to allow my life to be paralyzed by fear any longer and I reject fear out of my mind and body in Jesus Name. Father grant me the ability to release hurt, pain, shame, anger, rejection or any other negative emotion that have hindered my ability to love myself and walk in love. Help me to walk in love and with all the redemption power and benefits I have through Jesus Christ. In the name of Jesus. It is written, I walk in power, love and a sound mind and it cannot be otherwise.

8. **Isaiah 53:5 But he was wounded for our transgressions, he was bruised for our iniquities: the chastisement of our peace was upon him; and with his stripes we are healed.** Heavenly Father, because of what your son Jesus Christ did

on the cross please forgive me of my transgressions and iniquities and enforce my healing and deliverance in every way, for by the stripes of Lord Jesus Christ, healing is my portion. In the name of Jesus I am healed and claim my victory!

9. **Isaiah 43:18-19 18 Remember ye not the former things, neither consider the things of old.19 Behold, I will do a new thing; now it shall spring forth; shall ye not know it? I will even make a way in the wilderness, and rivers in the desert.** Father in the name of Jesus, as I move forward in your will for my life, I release the former shames, pains, blame, mistakes, negative cycles of…and excuses of my past. Father in the name of Jesus, do a new thing in my life— mind, body, spirit and soul, that my thinking, language, vocabulary and words will be in alignment of that which you O, Lord have said

concerning me and my abilities in Christ Jesus. Father paralyze every plot of oppression, pain, calamity and hardship that the devil will try to bring. And as your word is a lamp unto my feet and light unto my path, make a way for me if I am in the wilderness and provide rivers if I am in the desert.

10. **Romans 8: 11-16 ¹¹But if the Spirit of him that raised up Jesus from the dead dwell in you, he that raised up Christ from the dead shall also quicken your mortal bodies by his Spirit that dwelleth in you. Therefore, brethren, we are debtors, not to the flesh, to live after the flesh. ¹³For if ye live after the flesh, ye shall die: but if ye through the Spirit do mortify the deeds of the body, ye shall live. ¹⁴For as many as are led by the Spirit of God, they are the sons of God. ¹⁵For ye have not received the**

spirit of bondage again to fear; but ye have received the Spirit of adoption, whereby we cry, Abba, Father. [16]The Spirit itself beareth witness with our spirit, that we are the children of God: I am a (son/daughter) child of God. The same spirit that raised Jesus Christ from the dead is quickening me. Let the spirit of God heal and restore me and caste out every form of fear.

11. **1 John 5:4-5 [4]For whatsoever is born of God overcometh the world: and this is the victory that overcometh the world, even our faith. [5]Who is he that overcometh the world, but he that believeth that Jesus is the Son of God?** In the name of Jesus Christ I am born of God and believe in Jesus Christ. Through Jesus Christ I overcome every problem, hindrance, and difficulty of this world. I command the power of God to empower

me to overcome every challenge permanently.

12. **Psalm 34:19 ¹⁹ Many are the afflictions of the righteous: but the Lord delivereth him out of them all.** In the name of Jesus Christ I am the righteous of God through Jesus Christ. Thank you lord that you deliver me from all afflictions. The Lord Jesus is my shield and buckler, I will not be afraid! For I know that no weapon of the enemy formed against me shall prosper. My enemies may rise against me one way but they will flee from me in seven different ways.

13. **John 1:12 But as many as received Him (Jesus Christ) to him he gave the power to become the sons of God, even unto them that believe on his name:** I am a child of God. I receive Jesus Christ and believe.

14. **2 Corinthians 5:21 For he hath made him to be sin for us, who knew no sin; that we might be made the righteousness of God in him.** I am the righteousness of God in Jesus Christ. Christ in me the hope of glory.

15. **Romans 8:16-18 [16]The Spirit itself beareth witness with our spirit, that we are the children of God: [17]And if children, then heirs; heirs of God, and joint-heirs with Christ; if so be that we suffer with him, that we may be also glorified together. [18] For I reckon that the sufferings of this present time are not worthy to be compared with the glory which shall be revealed in us.** I am a child of God; a joint heir of Jesus Christ. I have a great inheritance of power, good things, goodness, mercy, wealth and riches.

16. **Luke 11:28 But he said, Yea rather, blessed are they that hear the word of God, and keep it.** Heavenly father, grant me the grace to move in obedience; to hear the word of God and keep it. Let your word become deeply rooted inside of me, that I may grow and always obtain victory, in every area of my life, in Jesus' name.

17. **John 15 4-5 [4]Abide in me, and I in you. As the branch cannot bear fruit of itself, except it abide in the vine; no more can ye, except ye abide in me. [5]I am the vine, ye are the branches: He that abideth in me, and I in him, the same bringeth forth much fruit: for without me ye can do nothing.** I am in Christ Jesus and Jesus Christ is in me. Heavenly father, help me to be a producer of good fruit. If you find anything inside of my thoughts, heart, body or soul that was not planted by you, remove it in Jesus' Name.

18. **Isaiah 54:17 No weapon that is formed against thee shall prosper; and every tongue that shall rise against thee in judgment thou shalt condemn. This is the heritage of the servants of the Lord, and their righteousness is of me, saith the Lord.** I am the righteous of God through Jesus Christ. I decree, any weapon, known and unknown, that the enemy forms against my life, family, husband, wife, children, health, mind, emotions, finances, purpose, calling and prosperity, shall not prosper. My life, health and strength are in the hands of God and He is a shield of protection for me and my household. God is my protection, even against any negative tongue or voice speaking against my life. Every wrong word or voice speaking against my life, I condemn, in Jesus' Name.

19. **Matthew 9:20-21 And, behold, a woman, which was diseased with an issue of blood twelve years, came behind him, and touched the hem of his garment: For she said within herself, If I may but touch his garment, I shall be whole.** Father, as the woman was healed with the issue of blood, I know healing is my portion. No matter how long I have been with this affliction, today is a new day. Father by your power that healed the woman with an issue that seemed impossible, locate me today. In the name of Jesus, I request that your healing power overflows through my total body, including my mind, spirit and soul. Let every long term battle that has been challenging my life come to an end. Grant me the grace to touch the hem of Jesus, for I know that through Jesus Christ, I am healed and made whole, Amen.

20. **Isaiah 40:31 But they that wait upon the Lord shall renew their strength; they shall mount up with wings as eagles; they shall run, and not be weary; and they shall walk, and not faint.** Lord, my life is in your hands. In my weakness you are made strong. Thank you for renewing my mind, health, joy and strength. I shall run the race and not be weary, walk towards the mark of your high calling and not faint.

Chapter 1
WHAT IS DELIVERANCE?

Un-Stuckness

There is no way to discuss deliverance without including salvation. Being delivered and saved goes hand in hand. When one is saved, he or she is delivered from a troubling dilemma through means of a rescue. Simultaneously, when one is delivered he is saved. A lifeguard cannot put his life in danger in the process of trying to rescue anyone. When someone is drowning, he has to be in a state of yielding to receive help.

In the process of performing a rescue, a lifeguard always has to communicate by announcing his presence and approach procedures before making physical contact with the victim. If a drowning person declines help, the lifeguard will stay with the victim but will not grab him until he is in agreement to receive help; otherwise the lifeguard's own life could be placed at risk. A lifeguard must be trained and every move must be made with knowledge, wisdom and understanding to preserve his own life from injury while saving another.

Keys to Deliverance through Prayer Jesus' Way

Unfortunately, some people may appear to be sinking and in need of someone to rescue them but are content with the battles and hardship of their current way of life. Because life has been nothing but darkness and one hardship after another, they have no desire to change or improve their life; they see change as hopeless.

But on the other hand, those that are drowning by any type of oppression will yield to be saved regardless of what they look like, what they have, who is watching, listening, or judging. They want to live and not die. And even if they sunk under and water got in their lungs, they badly want to be resuscitated so that they can breathe again and live— they want to be saved!

JESUS CHRIST IS THE ONLY ONE WHO SAVES

People in this category would welcome the door to experience salvation through Jesus Christ and His delivering power without hesitation. Jesus Christ is the only savior. Man was created to live in the presence of God. When being tempted by the devil, Adam disobeyed God and ate from the tree of the knowledge of good and evil. This disobedience created an entry to sin and a separation that removed man from the presence of God, in which we were designed by God to live, move and have our being (Genesis 3; Acts 17:28).

Jesus came on man's bond to destroy the works of Satan and restore back to mankind the opportunity to live in the presence of God (John 3:8). We were not made to live outside of God; in God is life but outside of God is death. What Adam did brought unto the world the Law of Sin and Death but what Jesus Christ did for us in the world, established the Law of the Spirit of life and broke the power of sin and death (Romans 5:12-21; Galatians 3:13).

Where the spirit of the Lord is there is liberty! Jesus restored mankind and provided us with power and authority to have life and have it more abundantly (John 10:10). With this authority, born-again believers through Jesus Christ have power over all the works of Satan (Luke 10:19-21). Satan

Keys to Deliverance through Prayer Jesus' Way

(the enemy) does not want you to have a life experiencing the good things of God. He wants you to be miserable and will aim to steal, kill and destroy your life by any means. Knowing that whatever trouble you may be facing today, Jesus Christ has the power to restore, heal, and deliver anyone who is dealing with any type of oppression.

ACCEPTING SALVATION

Accepting salvation (being saved) through Jesus Christ is the only way to receive deliverance (becoming rescued) from demonic attacks and strongholds. Those that accept Jesus Christ and call on the name of the Lord Jesus Christ will be saved (Acts 2:21; Romans 10: 9-13). By the Spirit of adoption through Jesus Christ, the spirit of bondage (that creates fear, yokes and strongholds) breaks (Romans 8:15). The power of Jesus Christ brings deliverance to everything concerning your life and soul. And a lifestyle of prayer sustains it.

Un-Stuckness

Those who accept salvation through Jesus Christ becomes children of God adopted into the family of Jesus Christ, saved by grace through faith (Ephesian 1: 3-6; Ephesians 2: 8-9; Galatians 3: 26-28; John 3: 14-17; Romans 8: 9-17). Remember, Jesus came that we will have life and have life more abundantly (John 10:10). They are then at the time of acceptance of His salvation, disconnected from the Law of sin and death and brought into the Law of the Spirit of Life (Romans 8:1).

A powerful transformation is made during acceptance; a pulling of one out from within the kingdom of darkness (where the enemy rules) and a transferring into the kingdom of light (where Jesus is King and Lord and rules over all). Whenever someone accepts Jesus Christ as their Lord and Savior, He becomes Lord and Savior of their life and everything contending with their rights and inheritance under the kingdom of God has no choice but to bow at the name of Jesus.

The transfer from one kingdom into another brings a transformation and the transformation changes everything: a new mind, heart, language, character, appearance and gives power over all the works of Satan (Romans 8:6-11; Luke 10:19). For if any man be in Jesus Christ, he becomes a new man. The old man of the flesh dies and the new man of the spirit is brought to life. "Therefore if any man be in Christ, he is a new creature: old things have passed away; behold all things are become new" (2 Corinthians 5:17). Sincerely accepting Jesus Christ to be Lord and Savior of your life is the first step to being saved.

When you accept salvation, you give God permission to guide the direction of your life, address everything good (prosperity) and bad (danger, hardships, lack, confusion, etc.) in your life and fight for you. God becomes your everything, your great shepherd, Jehovah Rapha (God that heals), Jehovah Shalom (your peace), Jehovah Jireh (your provider), Jehovah Tsidkenu (your righteousness) and more.

Salvation, truth, way, life, wisdom, knowledge, understanding, deliverer, helper, protector, friend, mother, father, husband, judge, defender, avenger, teacher, counselor, medicine and strength; ark of safety and strong tower. You are not leading yourself, but allowing the Lord and savior Jesus Christ to be the head of your life.

WHAT YOU MAY NEED DELIVERANCE FROM

On a frequent basis we all need deliverance of some sort, regardless of title, position, background and experience. Considering the diverse challenges that life brings, spiritual filtration is definitely needed from being overwhelmed, rude people, negative words, undesirable experiences and thoughts linked to regrets, anger and shame, and effects from the enemy attacks when we are most vulnerable. This is why, daily, it is important to ask God to deliver us from evil in every way and protect us from all plots and schemes of the enemy.

When individuals are fully aware of the path they need and desire to take **but cannot control** their behavior, deliverance is needed. In this type of situation, **internal mental and emotional factors** dominate and one feels powerless in making the necessary changes required to break a habit (that seems extremely difficult to stop).

One may also need deliverance from **external factors**, such as patterns that frequently occur which stop a blessing or makes life extremely difficult (situations related to employment, finances, health and relationships). Anyone who wants to break barriers that are causing setbacks and delays and gain control of their lives, instead of letting certain routines, habits, emotions dictate the quality of their life, would want to experience deliverance.

Additionally, when one is experiencing **any type of sickness** related to health, whether it be physical, mental, spiritual or emotional, deliverance is the result of a matter bring resolved. It brings joy, freedom, liberation, healing and peace of mind.

Un-Stuckness

WAYS YOU CAN YOU DEFINE DELIVERANCE

Deliverance is a separation process that saves and brings personal liberation and freedom from a bad situation or experience; a process that assists individuals to experience freedom, an enhanced quality of life, overcome mental and spiritual difficulties and gain clarity when planning and making decisions. This leads to the attainment of freedom or release from mental, physical, emotional or financial captivity.

It can also be defined as a successful outcome in which a person experiences a spiritual or emotional **release** and **freedom** from some type of negative feeling, emotion, addiction, spirit, behavior or habit that keeps one mentally, spiritually, emotionally, physically or financially in bondage, by overriding individual free will.

Anyone who wants to improve and gain control over their life instead of letting certain routines, habits or emotions dictate their life decisions and choices is desiring deliverance

Keys to Deliverance through Prayer Jesus' Way

(freedom). The benefit of deliverance is liberation, clarity and clear decision- making, an enhanced quality of life, the ability to overcome and accomplish goals, and the ability to release things that once kept you stuck. It also brings joy, inner peace and comfort.

People may need deliverance in the category of forgiveness, releasing the past, guilt, shame, stress rejection, blame, emotional pains (anger, rage, sadness, depression, self-loathing), drug addictions, sex addictions, stealing, lying, laziness, childhood abuse, past or present effects from unhealthy relationships, physical abuse, mental abuse, mental illness or verbal abuse.

The aforementioned issues listed can be a root problem or symptom that prevents an individual from living a fulfilled life, further hindering him or her from achieving his or her greatest potential. **Lack of deliverance** can make one experience so many sicknesses. That is why it becomes so important to welcome the great power of Jesus Christ to strip off negative weights, habits and issues that overpower individual free will to make a positive change. Otherwise challenges will become a long-term unending battle.

Even one issue can contribute to many additional physical, mental and emotional sicknesses. For example, depression is a health problem that impacts one's emotions and moods and can contribute to stomach ulcers, heart problems, sleep disorders, and memory loss. This shows that depression is a root problem that can multiply into many others.

TWO MAIN ISSUES WORTH EXAMINING

Do you know that if you can experience deliverance in areas linked to love and forgiveness, your life would experience healing and transformation on multiple levels. Mutually, love and forgiveness are two areas that deliverance is primarily needed in most people's lives. They are two issues a lot of people often struggle with the most. Unaddressed, they are seeds that grow into roots, branches and create many more additional negative problems on a mental, emotional, physical and spiritual level.

Thus, these issues become doorways for the enemy to manipulate and control one's quality of life. Nothing good can come from holding onto things that should have been dealt with and released.

The examples on the following chart shows how negative issues, experiences and situations can create a chain reaction, that can lead one to endure added mental distress that leads to emotional sickness that leads to physical sickness that leads to spiritual bondage; resulting in stagnation.

The good news is that deliverance can reverse sickness and bring restoration and healing to the body, mind, spirit and soul. Through Jesus Christ those who accept Jesus have a right to be healed and made whole. He is able to repair and address every area in which you have been attacked and wounded.

ROOT PROBLEM	OTHER ISSUES
Love	Lack of happiness and ambition, low self-esteem, rejection, identity issues, depression, anger, stress, envy, bitterness, hatred, anxiety, fear, trust, neglect, attachment, insecurity, craving to be accepted or needed, jealousy, emotional eating habits, weight problems, tolerance for staying in abusive or unhealthy relationships, unable to keep good relationships and heart problems.
Forgiveness	Resentment, anger, hate, rage, stress, mental torment, anxiety concentration difficulties, aggression, post-traumatic stress disorder, blame, shame, frustrations, depression, heart problems, high blood pressure, respiratory issues, alcohol and drug addiction; relationship issues and stagnation.

Keys to Deliverance through Prayer Jesus' Way

DELIVERANCE BRINGS HEALING

Spiritual bondages can only be addressed with spiritual solutions and approaches that have the ability to override negative effects. Spiritual solutions require welcoming salvation, intense prayer and study of the word of God—Spiritual medicine that leads to the elimination, healing and dissolving of negative symptoms and side effects.

Deliverance has the ability to heal the mind, body, spirit and soul. Having a willpower and desire to change the direction of your life into a better path is key to receiving that which you are asking, knocking and seeking. Seek help from God in spirit and in truth.

Deliverance, especially in love and forgiveness (these two areas), would most likely allow you to experience a more enhanced life that is centered around a foundation of peace that only walking in deliverance through Christ Jesus can bring. People, situations, and events will not be able to control and manipulate your internal peace, joy and calmness.

Negative experiences, issues and situations that are not addressed can lead to emotional, mental and physical sickness that have spiritual effects. A spiritual approach, anchored with the power of God has the ability to override the negative effects that lack of love and forgiveness has caused thus, leading to the illumination, healing and dissolvent of negative symptoms and negative side effects.

When you accept Jesus Christ as your Lord and Savior, everything that once had a grip on your peace and ability to prosper and be in good health has no choice but to leave and grant you your deliverance. The purging process will begin.

You may experience deliverance in one area before you receive it in another. Total deliverance may not happen immediately. God can move any way He determines is best for you and your learning process. When you are growing in your

Keys to Deliverance through Prayer Jesus' Way

relationship with God, He is always teaching and we are always learning, with every experience.

Our lessons may range from learning to trust and have faith in God, understanding kingdom principles, not being anxious and learning patience and time, to name a few. If total deliverance is given before we are ready to walk, we may quickly fall and the fall may be much harder to get up from.

Therefore, deliverance may come only on the level we are able to receive it through faith at the present time. God will not give something we are not ready to receive. Therefore, God will take you through one level of deliverance to the next. Victory to victory. Testimony to testimony.

The enemy is upset and feels like a failure every time a person is delivered from his kingdom of darkness into God's Kingdom of Light. The enemy does not want you to experience freedom from his oppression; because he has a legal right to manipulate your life when you hold onto negative feelings, emotions and behaviors. He does not want you to be saved and accept salvation, because salvation brings deliverance…evidence that he has lost and his stronghold on your life has been broken.

He does not want you to know God. He does not want you to have faith and trust God. He does not want you to know your power and authority over his works through Jesus Christ. He does not want you to have a strong prayer life. He does not want you to study and know the word of God. He does not want you to prosper, flourish or thrive at anything!

For all of these reasons, once you receive salvation it is important to know that the enemy will challenge you. What the enemy does want is for you to entertain fear, worry, doubt, be distracted, confused, run to man for help before running to God, miss your divine timing and never receive your goods. The enemy will create many bad situations but God has given you power to speak to every mountain.

The enemy will turn your friends into enemies or circle you around a mass of individuals who do not mean you well. He will judge and condemn you and get you to judge yourself. He will lie on you, attack your character and aim to hurt you through people; even those that you once looked up to. These experiences are nothing more than the enemy challenging your faith. His goal is for you to lose hope and remain in a discouraged state. He is a father of lies and deceit, and manipulation is what he does best.

The enemy operates by your physical sight and God operates by your faith. Hebrews 11:1 defines faith as "the substance of things hoped for the evidence of things not seen." How you react to negative news and situations is important! Therefore, it is wise to not make quick decisions and complete determinations based on how things naturally look to you. Have faith! What you see may not be the full truth and you can become upset and discouraged for nothing. Some things are just a trick of the enemy.

The devil is dirty and he does not have moral values and ethics. He will try to make you give up, quit and go backwards but I am writing you today to tell you the devil is a liar. His goal is for you to reject God and give up. When these events happen do not be shocked or surprised, STAND and keep your faith and trust in God. All you have to do is speak the word of God to every situation and don't be moved by what the physical eyes may see and report the ears hear.

PROTECT YOUR DELIVERANCE

If you give up and reject God the enemy would do his best to ensure you do not seek salvation again. He will aim to put you in a worse state than the first because he does not want you choosing entry back into the kingdom of light. Healing and deliverance are benefits of God's love mercy and grace. You have to do everything to maintain your deliverance.

There are things that can pull us close to God and there are things that can pull us away from Him. When the Lord delivers you from an issue,

Keys to Deliverance through Prayer Jesus' Way

you also have to protect your deliverance by refusing to engage in the wrong activities, listening to the wrong music, movies or TV shows or reading the wrong books. In addition, the wrong people, conversation, gossip, lies, jealousy, pride and selfishness can pull you from God and towards sin and the world. You have to watch what your eyes see, ears hear, head thinks and mouth speaks!

If you do not protect the gates connected to your head the enemy will enter back into your life. He will enter in by anything connected to sin. A sincere choice has to be made whether to yield towards God or yield to sin and worldly things. The wrong engagement can yield you towards sin and repel you from the things of God. And the WOW part is, the devil comes as a thief so quiet you won't even know he came.

You will find yourself in a mess and will not even know how it happened; just by entertaining the wrong things. The good news is that God is married to the backslider (Jeremiah 3:14). He will never reject your repentance and request for forgiveness and help to start over. God loves you despite your mistakes, falls and setbacks and there is nothing you can do to stop His love; the sun shines on the just as well as the unjust. His love shines even if you may fall; so get up and try again.

You cannot experience an enhanced un-stuck life filled with abundance, peace, achievements, accomplishments and good things, stuck in negativity that ties you up and restricts your ability to have emotional and mental freedom along with spiritual elevation. A decision concerning the quality of your life must be made. Do you want to remain stuck in the same mess and cycles or do you want to move forward into a greater level in life?

If you want to move forward there are changes and choices you must make that may not be easy. At the crosswalk between moving forward and remaining stuck, you have to choose the direction that will lead to the final destination you desire, even if it does not feel good. As you continue into the next chapters you will understand why utilizing

Keys to Deliverance through Prayer Jesus' Way

the Lord's prayer as a daily part of prayer is good for experiencing deliverance and maintaining it.

Chapter 2
GOOD ADVICE

Un-Stuckness

Romans 8:14-19

[14] For as many as are led by the Spirit of God, they are the sons of God. [15] For ye have not received the spirit of bondage again to fear; but ye have received the Spirit of adoption, whereby we cry, Abba, Father. [16] The Spirit itself beareth witness with our spirit, that we are the children of God: [17] And if children, then heirs; heirs of God, and joint-heirs with Christ; if so be that we suffer with [him], that we may be also glorified together. [18] For I reckon that the sufferings of this present time [are] not worthy [to be compared] with the glory which shall be revealed in us. [19] For the earnest expectation of the creature waiteth for the manifestation of the sons of God.

Keys to Deliverance through Prayer Jesus' Way

Children of God should be distinguished from the children of the world. The saved from the unsaved, those in darkness and those in light. This chapter will share a brief synopsis of important points you should know as you are embracing the characteristics and new nature of a child of God, so every thing positive remains closed to the enemy.

When God delivers and saves, there should be a new mindset. A new way to think, a new way to pray, a new way to live and a new way to treat your enemies; ways that reflect the fruit of God. Embracing a new and changed mind is the route to experiencing a transformed life (Romans 12:2).

A. MENTAL ATTITUDE

1. Accept Jesus Christ as your Lord and Savior. Believe in the Father who art in Heaven, the resurrected Son, Jesus Christ and the Holy Spirit (comforter). Have a strong desire to seek God with your total being.

2. Believe, trust God and have faith.

3. Repent of sins known and unknown (for yourself and your family).

4. Forgive yourself and those who have offended and wronged you (this includes in the past and on a present and daily basis).

5. Denounce wrongful engagements and activities (from yourself and your family, known and unknown). And disconnect yourself from negative influences.

6. Renew your mind daily. A transformed mind leads to a transformed life; be consistent and persistent. The right mental attitude is everything. Your mindset will impact your journey (Proverbs 23:7).

B. FOLLOW JESUS CHRIST'S NEW COMMANDMENT
(Matthew 22: 36-40)

Keys to Deliverance through Prayer Jesus' Way

1. Love God with all of your might, heart and soul. Be sincere with seeking and reaching an intimate relationship with God.

2. Love thy neighbor. Love people, even when they act their worst, it's a spirit behind the worst of the worst. The spirit causing the behavior is our true enemy. We have to think as Jesus did when they hung him on the cross, "He said forgive them Father because they know not what they do (Luke 23:34)."

3. Also, this same attitude is necessary when dealing with people who are not so easy to love; they know not what they do. Jesus' new commandment was LOVE. Love is the Greatest Power and supersedes any spiritual gift.

C. POWER OF LOVE

1. Love breaks all types of yokes and bondages. It is also why it is so important to practice what

Un-Stuckness

Jesus taught, which is to pray for your enemies and those who spitefully use you.

2. When people that never received love are truly loved, their outlook inwardly and outwardly can change and bring deliverance.

3. Love never fails and for this reason Satan tries to place limits on our capacity to love and receive love. If Satan can control our ability to love and receive love, he controls our life, peace, joy, quality of life and relationship with God.

4. Thus, expanding your ability to leave judgment of others up to God is one way that will keep you from being bound by enemy manipulations and allow you to love.

5. Otherwise, bitterness, anger, resentment, un-forgiveness, envy and hatred can enter your spirit and these are all of Satan's friends; if you

let them in, you let him in! When they are evicted, he is also evicted.

6. They are tactics used to connect you to Satan's manipulations like a puppet, giving him permission in your life and it is vital that we do not allow him access, especially easy access. Do you want to remain free or not? This is the main question you have to ask yourself.

7. Every day you should detox yourself from anything the enemy can use against you and ask God to help your weaknesses become your strengths.

8. The way you love, treat and pray for people, especially those that don't like you (regardless of family title or relationship) must be genuine.

9. It takes a desire for spiritual maturity and desire to do what's right in the eyes of God to

pray for your enemies' deliverance and not just your own.

D. SEEK FRIST THE KINGDOM OF GOD AND ITS RIGHTEOUSNESS

1. Proverbs 3:6 says if you acknowledge God in all your ways, He will direct your path. Keep God first in every aspect of your decision making: how to worship, how to pray, personal goals, career, relationships, child rearing and disciplining, conflicts, crisis situations, vacations, shopping, budget, even the clothes you put on.

2. God should be first before you start your day; in prayer, scripture reading and meditation. In addition, He should be first in giving your tithes (10% of your first fruits). In tithing, God will bless you and devour the enemy (Malachi 3:10-11), in loving and honoring God you should always have the nature of giving Him your first in all you do.

3. Acknowledging God in everything will assist with developing a beneficial disciplined mentality. There is nothing wrong with asking God for guidance, directions, protection and favor and to place your angels on assignment to counteract any plot of the enemy.

4. Keeping God first minimizes the enemy's ability to manipulate your life and gives you an advantage over him. The more you keep God first, the more in tune you will be with hearing and feeling God's directions concerning your life.

5. Keeping God first in everything will make it challenging for Satan to easily have an advantage over you. You will not be permanently stuck in storms, repeating cycles or strongholds. Whoever God sets free is free indeed if you keep Him first in your life.

6. This doesn't eliminate the experience of trials and tribulations; it just means that as you keep

your eyes, faith and trust in God no matter what, you will come out victorious and spiritually stronger. God does not lead His sheep blindly.

7. Even if you don't personally know which way to go, don't let that turn into worry. It is not your place to know all the details of how God is moving, changing and addressing the matter; it is your place to just have faith and trust God.

8. Jesus said "I am the way, the truth and the life (John 14:6)." So long as you keep your mind and steps in tune with keeping God first, your way will be made and your life will be blessed.

9. The word of the Lord is your truth. God's word and promises for your life are your protection during a storm, trial or tribulation. Enforce what is true by making declarations and decrees, taking strong positions of authority that your life will be what God says and not otherwise! Any other picture or

thoughts opposite of this is a lie. You will reap according to your belief.

10. Remember Satan is the Master of Lies and always aims to make the children of God waiver in faith by presenting a false picture or illusion to our sight, lies to our ears and spreading a smell of fear. Besides touch, all the other senses are connected to your head. The head is the most vulnerable part of the body, physically, spiritually and must always be protected. The physical body cannot function adequately with a damaged or injured head. The same is true spiritually.

11. God has called His children to be the head and not the tail. If your spiritual head/mind is left vulnerable and unprotected, you cannot be spiritually and mentally strong in the Lord and operate in the power of His might.

12. It is important to not let the arrows of the enemy hit your head. When the enemy targets

your head, it is only for one purpose, to kill and destroy your spiritual mind and spiritual health (stability) and as a result, hope that you will become spiritually dead or sick; destroyed.

13. A mind that has been spiritually wounded will incur spiritual symptoms (associated with fear and confusion) that do not line up with the word of God. It also has the ability to separate and disconnect your walk with God by making one double-minded. Always protect your head with the helmet of salvation.

14. The helmet of salvation and shield of faith must be strongly intertwined in your daily walk. Your head and all organs connected to it must be protected by all means. Don't leave it defenseless to attacks. Build it up and keep it strong fed with the right foods. The body cannot operate without the head, so let God be the head in your life.

15. Our spiritual sight must supersede the physical sight. TRUTH will set us free; so, what report are you going to believe? The Devil (Satan) operates with deception, making something look real or like it is the truth when it actually is far from the truth or real. His greatest accomplishment in the lives of Christians is to bring confusion and division into the body of Christ and into the homes of families. When we learn how to stay in unity and love, the harder it will be for the enemy to steal, kill and bring destruction into our lives.

E. POWER IN UNITY

1. There is power in unity and the kingdom of darkness knows this. For instance, this is why when one demon is cast out of a body it attempts to come back with 7 more demons stronger than himself (Luke 11:24-26; Matt. 12:43-45). For this reason, when you receive

deliverance over any area, KEEP IT and PROTECT IT!

2. The enemy brings more demons to accomplish a collective goal (which is to destroy) to take you over. Demonic rank or title do not interfere or become in conflict with them collectively working together in an effort to obtain a desired outcome. In other words, they don't argue or debate on who is the stronger or better demon when trying to dominate your temple.

3. We must learn how to be one body in Christ as children of God (Galatians 3:26-28; 1 Corinthians 12:12-13) and stand against operating with the spirit of division. Not being more concerned about rank, title, position and gifts, than following Jesus' principles on love and unity; so that souls would be saved, delivered and set free. The enemy is happy when children of God operate in division and confusion.

4. Operating with the spirit of division brings weakness. Even our families and relationships are weakened when division is present. The hand of God works strongly with the spirit of unity. When your spirit is in unity with His, you will prosper. On the other hand, when division is present you will fail.

5. Regardless of your situation, GOD always has the last say and no matter what things look like, I am sure that the situation you may be facing is not final. There's still an opportunity for change, and it is not the end; however, Satan would make you believe that it is.

F. EMBRACING KEEPING GOD FIRST

1. For this reason, it is vital to always and daily let your mind be renewed. Renew by affirming what the word of God says about who you are, what you can do (power and authority) and your privileges. In knowing who you are, you

will not entertain the things that you are not. The scriptures tell us, the way to be transformed is by the renewing of your mind. This process builds mental and spiritual stamina, especially when done with diligence, consistency and routinely.

2. So, as you embrace a life of keeping God first, "diligently" in all you do, it will become evident that your spiritual food is just as vital for spiritual nourishment, as your physical food is for physical nourishment of the natural body.

3. Every day it is necessary to partake your daily bread (the word of God) and drink (the Blood of Jesus) spiritually and physically (actual communion). For as Jesus taught, man cannot live by bread alone but by every word that proceeds out of the mouth of God. He desires that we partake communion often as we think of it (Mark 14:22-25; Luke 22:18-20; 1 Corinthians 11:23-25).

Keys to Deliverance through Prayer
Jesus' Way

4. As you let God direct your path, choices and will, your way will be made for He will direct your way. He will bring you out of the wilderness and dark places, with victory and a greater anointing!

5. He will bring you out of every trial and tribulation with endurance, patience and strength! Some situations and issues are extremely difficult to get over, but with God on your side Victory will be your name! He is more than capable to heal your life and make you whole. Only the creator can fix its creation, the creation can't repair itself.

6. Surrender your all to God. Resting on the complete trust of man to make your brokenness or hurt transition into wholeness, completeness and/or restoration, is like mission impossible. Broken people cannot fix your pieces and put you back together again. Even relying on helpers that may have it

somewhat together cannot restore you completely.

7. Only the great physician can do that which is impossible by man. You must seek your Maker, Father, Healer, Lord and Savior. The ONE who created life, and has all life in His hands is more than capable to deliver you out of every form of mental, emotional and physical bondage.

8. Train yourself to pursue and connect with God's opinion first, concerning various issues. Seek Him foremost before running to man. If God is using man to help you, still keep Him first in it.

9. This will ensure that God will remain your God and man will not become a replica. Your trust in man should never supersede that of God. Jeremiah 17:5 talks about how unfortunate one's life can become by trusting man more than God. What can stand up against Our

Mighty God and win? NOTHING!!! Believe, seek and trust Him. The word of God says that if you acknowledge God in all your ways He will direct your path (Proverbs 3:6).

10. God keeps those in perfect peace whose mind is stayed on Him. As you study, read, meditate and pray (daily and throughout the day) your mind, body, and soul will be in alignment with THE TRUTH. As a man thinks so is he. Following God and His word gives delivery to True LIFE.

11. When you pray, follow the guidance of THE LORD'S PRAYER as a guide to address every area in your life (Matt 6: 9-13 & Luke 11: 2-4).

Chapter 3
THE KEYS TO DELIVERANCE

Un-Stuckness

The keys to deliverance are: repenting, confessing and releasing. Jesus directs us through these three steps in His demonstration of how to pray in Matthew and Luke (the Lord's Prayer). As you go through the process of praying The Lord's Prayer, it will take you through spiritual cleansing and purging stages; it should be prayed sincerely.

You cannot be completely delivered without embracing the three aforementioned keys, they must be used. The three keys can be used before reciting the Lord's Prayer or included during any type of prayer. However you decide to pray, be sure that the keys are applied on a daily basis.

Even though the Lord's Prayer takes you through each step of the three keys, you might not choose to recite the Lord's Prayer all the time. For this reason, the most important thing to know is that you are not restricted to the Lord's Prayer and can use the three keys every time you are led to pray in your own way.

Each step of the three keys initiates a releasing and healing process that removes spiritual contaminates, allowing the light and love of God to flow in places where there was darkness.

REPENT FROM SINS

Repenting from sins means that you have had a mind change and a change of heart. A mental change that reflects a lifestyle transformation of no longer operating as the old man but as a new man doing things a new way. The word repent deals with regretting a situation in which you feel sorry, shame or remorse and having a change in heart [remember as a man think in his heart so is he].

As a believer, it is essential to daily practice repenting and ask for forgiveness regarding things that were done in error, known or unknown (also know you can repent for yourself and others). Personally, I repent for my sins, parents, children, ancestors and those I want to intercede for in prayer. I maintain the same similar concept expressed in Leviticus 40-42. The method of repenting for your husband, wife, children, relatives and friends before starting the intercessory part of prayer, is a swift chain breaker. It contends with the enemy legal right over them and brings positive outcomes.

I have another book called *Un-Stuckness: Breaking Generational Chains and Strongholds Through Prayer*, that goes further and deeper on repenting for your family's lineage. Repenting can also be described as making an apology and sincerely being remorseful for what was transpired. This action shows that you seek forgiveness as well.

Jesus strongly emphasized repentance (Matthew 4:17). 2 Peter 3:9 states that Jesus' objective was that all should come into repentance so no one would have to perish; Jesus wanted us to have an abundant life. Further in Luke 13:3 an important link between repentance and death is made. It signifies that failure to repent can cause individuals to perish and remain stuck in darkness. When one is not drawn to repentance their heart is hardened. Luke reveals its importance.

Keys to Deliverance through Prayer Jesus' Way

Repentance is a key that will break the enemy's grip, grant you favor during prayer requests and allow you to have a liberated life in Christ. Refusing to repent is linked to pride, stubbornness, rebellion and that you don't need God [acceptance to sin]. When you repent, make a decision that you want to change. God examines your heart and sincerity. It's a very important first part linked to your cleansing process.

CONFESS YOUR SINS

To confess allows one to verbally express an event. During confession, a person openly informs a mistake, an offense, hurt or regrets. Confessing allow things of the dark to be brought into the light.

The enemy wants things to remain hidden in the dark so that he can have power, control and manipulation abilities, but when you allow matters to be exposed to the light, Satan loses his power. You can confess to God, a pastor or a safe individual.

Un-Stuckness

Confessing requires a willingness to remove the cover and expose situations, secrets and fault(s) into the light and place it in God's hands. When you confess, the releasing stage can start and things that once held you back, no longer have a stronghold on you; you will become able to break free and move forward.

When you confess, it allows you to confront and release your sins or sins personally impacting you from the actions of others. Additionally, it shows that you do not want to carry that negative weight on the inside any longer. The Scriptures say that if you confess your sins, God is just and faithful to forgive you and then clean you up from all unrighteousness (1 John 1:9).

This shows that confessing your sins before God is the process that will yield Him to then forgive and clean you of all spiritual contaminates that can make life very heavy. The word of God states in Romans 8:1 and 2 Corinthians 5:17, that there is no more condemnation for those who are in Christ Jesus, for all old things have passed way behold all things become new. He separates our sins as far as the east is from the west.

Confessing is a key that breaks the bands of strongholds associated with shame, resentment, regrets, failure, hurt, shame, blame etc. When you confess, things no longer have power over you, you gain power over it. God then becomes able to clean and repair; it's not the other way around. It's the second step to your cleansing process.

RELEASE YOUR SINS

After you confess, the releasing and purging process can start. This is the third step to deliverance. Releasing is associated with letting go and allowing something to leave. This part is strongly associated with forgiving yourself or another.

God commands His children to lay aside every weight (Hebrews 12:1). This is not always so easy to do but is required, if you want to become free. Releasing allows us to let go of things (regrets, shame and hurts) that would otherwise be heavy weights keeping us bound, stuck and unable to move forward.

A lot of people are stuck in their past because they refuse to release and let things which they have no control over, go. The inability to release keeps individuals in emotional, physical and spiritual bondage.

The enemy loves when people are in bondage because it restricts their prosperity, freedom, joy, health and peace in life. Living a life in bondage is no way to truly live.

Jesus died for the redeemed and born again to have an enriched life that would flourish, be fruitful, multiply and prosper, not to remain bound to sin and separated from God.

In general, sometimes we can be so hard on ourselves when we make mistakes, but God just wants us to try again and do better next time; he knows we fall short and are not perfect all the time.

Releasing permits you the ability to exhale darkness and inhale light. The releasing process is

Keys to Deliverance through Prayer Jesus' Way

successful when there is no more shame or blame to hold you back mentally and you truly and fully release ALL OF IT! This is why you must confess before the ability to release is impossible. Releasing is the final step and pathway to deliverance.

Jesus gives the best foundational guide on teaching us strategies for how to pray effectively in order to manifest change victoriously. Jesus Christ's guidance (Matt 6: 5-21 & Luke 11: 1-4) has two different versions with the same blueprint. Following Jesus' example of how we should pray takes you through a cleansing and renewing process as it is prayed. We need to be fed, cleaned, renewed, restored, and repaired daily, trust me!

The Lord's Prayer addresses every sector in your life that will mold you into being delivered, staying delivered, and having the attributes of strength, faith and trust in the Lord. If you engage, contemplate on what this prayer is really saying and pray is sincerely you will experience breakthrough, spiritual growth and maturity.

JESUS CHRIST'S TEACHINGS ON PRAYER

Matt 6:5-21 **⁵ And when thou prayest, thou shalt not be as the hypocrites are: for they love to pray standing in the synagogues and in the corners of the streets, that they may be seen of men. Verily I say unto you, They have their reward.** [Prayer is an intimate act and should not be done to portray a certain image before man but done because you value a relationship with God. It should be engaged with the right spirit and intent because you love and fear God.] **⁶ But thou, when thou prayest, enter into thy closet, and when thou hast shut thy door, pray to thy Father which is in secret; and thy Father which seeth in secret shall reward thee openly.** [Some people perceive that they need to make an actual closet but what Jesus was referring to is praying silently from within (a secret place between you and Him). Some prayers are more effective when you pray silently to your Heavenly Father and others are stronger when you use your mouth and speak; it depends on the season in your life and warfare.] **⁷ But when ye pray, use not vain repetitions, as the heathen do: for they think that they shall be heard for their much speaking. ⁸ Be not ye therefore like unto them: for your Father knoweth what things ye have need of, before ye ask him.** [Praying does not have to be a long process. Doing it sincerely from your heart in spirit and truth is what matters most.]

⁹ After this manner therefore pray ye: Our Father which art in heaven, Hallowed be thy name. ¹⁰ Thy kingdom come. Thy will be done in earth, as it is in heaven. ¹¹ Give us this day our daily bread. ¹² And forgive us our debts, as we forgive our debtors. ¹³ And lead us not into temptation, but deliver us from evil: For thine is the kingdom, and the power, and the glory, forever. Amen.

Un-Stuckness

KEY POINTS

1. Jesus' lifestyle was strongly centered on prayer. Matthew 6:9-13 reveals instructions Jesus gave His disciples on how to pray.
2. Each statement takes you through a cleansing phase and dimension in prayer. The order should not be skipped and this prayer should not be taken for granted.
3. It should be communed with sincerity, honesty, intensity, purpose and expectation.

[14] For if ye forgive men their trespasses, your heavenly Father will also forgive you: [15] But if ye forgive not men their trespasses, neither will your Father forgive your trespasses. [Reveals how un-forgiveness can interfere with your prayers] **[16] Moreover when ye fast, be not, as the hypocrites, of a sad countenance: for they disfigure their faces, that they may appear unto men to fast. Verily I say unto you, They have**

their reward. **¹⁷ But thou, when thou fastest, anoint thine head, and wash thy face; ¹⁸ That thou appear not unto men to fast, but unto thy Father which is in secret: and thy Father, which seeth in secret, shall reward thee openly.** [Explains the importance of letting your actions be intimate between you and God. Internal godly motives are not for the external image for men to see and judge.] **¹⁹ Lay not up for yourselves treasures upon earth, where moth and rust doth corrupt, and where thieves break through and steal: ²⁰ But lay up for yourselves treasures in heaven, where neither moth nor rust doth corrupt, and where thieves do not break through nor steal: ²¹ For where your treasure is, there will your heart be also.** [Jesus is emphasizing a previous message that through Him we have eternal life and that it is more beneficial to focus on the things that are eternal than carnal and temporary.]

Un-Stuckness

Luke 11:1-4(KJV)

¹ And it came to pass, that, as he was praying in a certain place, when he ceased, one of his disciples said unto him, Lord, teach us to pray, as John also taught his disciples.² And he said unto them, when ye pray, say, Our Father which art in heaven, Hallowed be thy name. Thy kingdom come. Thy will be done, as in heaven, so in earth.³ Give us day by day our daily bread.⁴ And forgive us our sins; for we also forgive every one that is indebted to us. And lead us not into temptation; but deliver us from evil.

Scriptures dealing with Confessing and Repentance: (Also Psalm 51 is good to read and pray when repenting)

Luke 13:5 I tell you, Nay: but, except ye repent, ye shall all likewise perish.

Romans 3:23 For all have sinned, and come short of the glory of God.

Keys to Deliverance through Prayer
Jesus' Way

1 John 1:9 If we confess our sins, he is faithful and just to forgive us [our] sins, and to cleanse us from all unrighteousness.

Romans 10:13 For whosoever shall call upon the name of the Lord shall be saved.

Isaiah 43:18 Remember ye not the former things, neither consider the things of old.

Acts 3:19 Repent ye therefore, and be converted, that your sins may be blotted out, when the times of refreshing shall come from the presence of the Lord;

2 Peter 3:9 The Lord is not slack concerning his promise, as some men count slackness; but is longsuffering to us-ward, not willing that any should perish, but that all should come to repentance.

Un-Stuckness

Matthew 4:17 From that time Jesus began to preach, and to say, Repent: for the kingdom of heaven is at hand.

Luke 15:10 Likewise, I say unto you, there is joy in the presence of the angels of God over one sinner that repenteth.

Acts 17:30 And the times of this ignorance God winked at; but now commandeth all men everywhere to repent:

1 John 1:8 If we say that we have no sin, we deceive ourselves, and the truth is not in us.

Ephesians 4:31-32 Let all bitterness, and wrath, and anger, and clamour, and evil speaking, be put away from you, with all malice:

Philippians 4:8-9 Finally, brethren, whatsoever things are true, whatsoever things [are] honest, whatsoever things [are] just, whatsoever things

Keys to Deliverance through Prayer Jesus' Way

[are] pure, whatsoever things [are] lovely, whatsoever things [are] of good report; if [there be] any virtue, and if [there be] any praise, think on these things.

Proverbs 28:13 He that covereth his sins shall not prosper: but whoso confesseth and forsaketh [them] shall have mercy.

Matthew 3:8 Bring forth therefore fruits meet for repentance:

James 5:16 Confess [your] faults one to another, and pray one for another, that ye may be healed. The effectual fervent prayer of a righteous man availeth much.

Romans 10:9 That if thou shalt confess with thy mouth the Lord Jesus, and shalt believe in thine heart that God hath raised him from the dead, thou shalt be saved.

Un-Stuckness

Matthew 9:13 13But go ye and learn what that meaneth, I will have mercy, and not sacrifice: for I am not come to call the righteous, but sinners to repentance.

Luke 15:7 I say unto you, that likewise joy shall be in heaven over one sinner that repenteth, more than over ninety and nine just persons, which need no repentance.

2 Chronicles 7:14 If my people, which are called by my name, shall humble themselves, and pray, and seek my face, and turn from their wicked ways; then will I hear from heaven, and will forgive their sin, and will heal their land.

Hebrews 12:1-2 [1]Wherefore seeing we also are compassed about with so great a cloud of witnesses, let us lay aside every weight, and the sin which doth so easily beset us, and let us run with patience the race that is set before us, [2]Looking unto Jesus the author and finisher of our faith; who

Keys to Deliverance through Prayer Jesus' Way

for the joy that was set before him endured the cross, despising the shame, and is set down at the right hand of the throne of God.

James 1:15 Then when lust hath conceived, it bringeth forth sin: and sin, when it is finished, bringeth forth death.

Joel 2:13 And rend your heart, and not your garments, and turn unto the LORD your God: for he is gracious and merciful, slow to anger, and of great kindness, and repenteth him of the evil.

Acts 2:38 Then Peter said unto them, Repent, and be baptized every one of you in the name of Jesus Christ for the remission of sins, and ye shall receive the gift of the Holy Ghost.

Titus 2:12 Teaching us that, denying ungodliness and worldly lusts, we should live soberly, righteously, and godly, in this present world.

Un-Stuckness

There is no way transformation can take place in your life, when you do not change your mind or strongly desire to operate differently. Your heart must be in agreement with your mind and desires as well. Otherwise, you will want change, but never take the necessary steps to make change happen.

Holding on to bad experiences, such as mistakes, shame, blame, guilt, anger and fear to name a few, can be very toxic to multiple areas of your health. When your mind and heart is sincere to let go of negative things, good things and new beginnings can take place; the choice is yours.

Keys to Deliverance through Prayer Jesus' Way

Repent

Confess

Release

Pray

Believe

Give Thanks

Praise

Chapter 4
DISSECTING THE LORD'S PRAYER

Un-Stuckness

Our Father, which art in Heaven. Address God as Father who art in Heaven, the creator of Heaven and earth and all life SINCERELY. **Hallowed be thy Name**. Holy is the name of the Lord. Acknowledges holy is our God.

Thy Kingdom come. Jesus preached many lessons on the kingdom of Heaven and made clear the kingdom of Heaven is at hand. He was given authority to operate in Heaven and Earth simultaneously. As joint heirs with Christ we have this same authority also. We have access to operate in God's Kingdom because as His children we are a part of it.

When we pray, we are asking the kingdom of Heaven (God) to assist us on earth with enforcing the word of God, Heavenly principles, assignment of Angels, and application of spiritual weaponry to enforce spiritual boundaries, limitations and restrictions. God's Kingdom is of light, we are children of light (John 12:35-36; 1 John 1:5-9; 1 Thessalonians 5:5), and must know the word of God, Heavenly laws, principles and legislations connected to the Kingdom of God, along with how to put them in action. Satan has a demonic kingdom of darkness, demons, evil spirits and principalities, over powers, over the rulers of the darkness of this world, over spiritual wickedness in high places (Ephesians 6:12).

For this reason, we need the kingdom of God/light/Heaven to come and stand in agreement with our words and prayers as we exercise our rights and authority against the Kingdom of Satan/darkness; God moves when we ask in prayer. Therefore, we position the kingdom of heaven to bring an alignment of what we decree on earth.

Thy will be done on earth. reminds us to submit our will to the Lord. We want the will of the Lord, embracing His way over our way and will. God has expectations for His children and we agree to walk and live according to His will.

As it is in Heaven. Jesus was given authority to operate in Heaven and Earth jointly; asking God to let His will concerning your life be aligned in Heaven and Earth concurrently.

Give us this day our daily bread. The word of God is our spiritual food. Jesus said that man cannot live alone but by every word that proceeds out of the mouth of God. This shows that we need the word of God to live spiritually. Our spirit is fed, nourished and strengthened by the word of God. So daily we need the word of God, to strengthen our spirit, and renew our mind and thoughts on the word of God.

In general, not eating the right foods can impact one's mind and ability to think clearly. The same is true if you don't eat right spiritually, your spiritual mind will be weakened and you will not have a sound mind or the mind of Christ the way God desires; the word of God strengthens the spirit and life of the children of God (Matt. 4:4; Deuteronomy 8:3; Roman 12:2; Philippians 2:5; 1corinthians 2:14-16; John 6:63; Exodus 16:8).

Also, Jesus commanded us eat of His flesh and drink of His blood for He is the bread of life. This is why taking communion daily signifies that you eat of the body of Jesus and drink of His blood and stand in agreement with His covenant and the redemption we all received through His sacrifice on the cross. Therefore, when you take communion you are agreeing that sickness is not your portion and no sin should possess your life and that by Jesus Christ you are healed and made whole.

And forgive us our trespasses. There's power in confessing our sins and seeking forgiveness for our faults known and unknown (1John 1:5-9). Confessing our sins breaks the enemy's hold and allows God to forgive and cleanse us.

As we forgive them that trespass against us. God wants us to have a mind of forgiving others, just as we would want to be forgiven (Ephesians 4:32; Matt 6:14; Colossians 3:13; Luke 6:37; Proverbs 28:13; Acts 3:19).

And lead us not into temptation. You want God to give you the power to avoid temptation, greed, anger, manipulations, arguments, demonic triggers and responding in the flesh. This allows you to have spiritual alertness; to have an attentive mind to watch and pray so you do not fall into temptation (James 1:2-3; James 1:12; Mark. 14:36; Matt. 26:41; Luke 22:40; Galatians 6:1; Proverbs 6:12-14).

We have to grow as children of God, to be able to resist temptations. God does not tempt his children. Being able to resist temptation strengthens our faith, patience and trust in God. There is power in resisting that causes the devil to flee (James 4:7).

But deliver us from evil. Ask God to deliver you from all evil, not some evil but all evil! God desires for His children to be clean. **For thine is the kingdom, the power, and the glory, forever and ever.** God is the Kingdom, God is Power and God is Glory and nothing can change this; God is the source of everything

Chapter 5
HOW TO PRAY JESUS' WAY

Un-Stuckness

Prayer is communication with God. This communication with God is not only routed to him in Heaven but on the inside of you and your atmosphere. The words that come out of your mouth through prayer are spirit and life. This is why Jesus says in Matthew 17: 20 that if you have faith the size of a mustard seed you can command a mountain to move from one place to another and it shall be removed; in addition, nothing shall be impossible. Prayer strengthens, heals, protects and allow you to intercede on all matters. What you say can move a lot of things or allow unwanted things to persist in your life. This is why, the word of God should be spoken to every situation concerning your life.

The word of God is a weapon (the sword) that fights in the spirit for you, it is a necessary part of the defense attire children of God must wear daily at all times (Ephesian 6:17; Hebrews 4:12). Having an open mouth for prayer and speaking the word of God is essential to remaining victorious. Children of God do not live by bread alone but by every word that proceeds out of the mouth of God (Matthew 4:4). When you pray using the word of God as suggested in the introduction of this book and in the example of the Lord's Prayer provided, the word of God becomes rooted on the inside of you. It is a mighty weapon; the shield and buckler of God protecting you from the darks of the enemy (Psalm 18:30).

The word of God will stand forever (Isaiah 40:8; Matthew 24:53) and when it is on the inside of you it will help you to stand! God watches over His word and it cannot return unto Him void. It has to accomplished that which He pleases (Jeremiah 1:12; Isaiah 55:11). So it is important to speak to every mountain that wants to intimidate and challenge your faith. Don't give attention to how bad or unmovable it appears before you, your job is to speak and command it out of your way.

Jesus said if you abide in me and my word abide in you, you can ask anything and it will be done for you that the father who art in Heaven will be glorified (John 15:7). When God's word is on the inside of you, you can ask anything. When you exercise your faith you can move mountains. Therefore, be persistent in prayer.

If you desire a release and breakthrough, follow the formula of the Lord's Prayer sincerely and your life will be transformed. It is an important reason why Jesus provided this example of how to pray. Please realize Jesus' way of teaching the disciples how to pray is a foundational frame of prayer for all believers. Jesus taught us the best way to effectively pray.

If the foundation be destroyed, what will the righteous do? Children of God must hold on to their foundation in Jesus Christ. Importantly, it is powerful and has the capability to renew, strengthen and purge you daily from any pollution that the enemy may try to bring into your spirit. As you daily and consistently pray in the format provided by Jesus, the ropes that kept you tied down and prevented you from moving forward will break.

Keys to Deliverance through Prayer Jesus' Way

Jesus' teaching on how to pray is the best prayer foundational guide you can ever use in life. He provided adequate instructions to keep you in the right standing with God and have favor during prayer. Incorporating it with part of your daily prayers will eliminate your feeling that you do not know how to pray or the assumption that you are praying in vain.

It is my recommendation that praying the Lord's Prayer should be daily, at the beginning of your praying process, especially before making any additional prayer requests. This will ensure that there is little chance of being denied because you did not make an effort to forgive, for an example. It closes and removes the enemy's power to keep you and your prayers stuck.

For this reason, it is essential to present yourself properly. When you come before the Lord, you must come with the right mind, attitude and a sincere heart— In Spirit and In Truth.

AN EXAMPLE OF HOW TO USE JESUS' PRAYER A GUIDE OF HOW JAMILLAH USES IT, CURTAILED JUST FOR YOU:

[9] **My Father which art in Heaven,** Hallowed be thy name. Holy are you Lord. [10] **Thy kingdom come, thy will be done in earth, as it is in Heaven** (confession). Father God, I seek first your kingdom and your righteousness in my life today. Let your kingdom come to assist me on earth. I operate with my God-given authority and dominion over the earth and request the kingdom of Heaven to manifest on the earth realm and operate freely, assisting me with achieving the things God desires for me to achieve and the things He has given me access to do with the greatest capacity. Let the Kingdom of Heaven fight for me today.

Fight for my purpose, will and destiny to line up with Jesus' desire for my life. Let your will be done in my life. Let the kingdom of Heaven fight against every dark cloud, gate or portal designed to hinder and make life difficult for me. Let the

Keys to Deliverance through Prayer Jesus' Way

Kingdom of Heaven fight against all forces of darkness, fighting my prayers, breakthrough, children, health, future, destiny, goals and glory.

I submit my will unto your will and decree that your will is my will, and my will your will. It is your will for me to be delivered, it is your will for me to prosper and be fruitful. It is your will for me to love you and I love you dearly Lord. I seek your face today. It is your will to be my protector and provider. It is your will for me to trust you. It is your will for me to walk in faith and not by sight. So, strengthen my faith today O, Lord; for you Lord are my Sheppard, and no good thing will you withhold to them that love you and diligently seek your face.

[11] Give me this day my daily bread (confession). O, Lord feed me today your word, manna from Heaven. Allow me to be fed with the bread of life that I may be spiritually nourished capable to grow, develop, mature and thrive strongly in you. Feed me the word that I need for this day and this season. Eliminate any food source planted by the enemy to hinder my growth and life. Feed my mind, spirit and soul today, dear Lord, for man cannot live by bread alone but by every word that proceeds out of your mouth.

Therefore, I come before you asking you to feed me your word so that I am strengthened and fueled with the right knowledge, wisdom and understanding to deal with people, situations and any challenges today may hold. Feed me the word that will counteract against the potential plot, scheme and wicked agenda of the enemy - the word that will fight for me.

Allow my mouth to be an equipped tool that will speak your word to every lie, mountain and mulberry tree in my path. Father, your word is alive, active and sharper than any two-edged sword and shall not return to you void. Lord, let your word cut, crush and destroy anything aiming to block my strength, growth, power and life in you today.

Let your words downpour knowledge, wisdom and understanding needed for this day that

Keys to Deliverance through Prayer Jesus' Way

I may not perish but live, succeed, flourish and prosper in you. Lord, it is only by the power of your word that I am strong in faith and standing on your mighty words.

¹² Father please forgive me of my debts, faults and trespasses (list them, things you have done, people you have offended. This is the confession/repenting process as well as things I have done wrong known and unknown). I seek your forgiveness and ask that you help me communicate and respond to others in a way that is humble and demonstrates love so that I won't offend or speak words that are not kind, even if they are unkind to me.

Father, I forgive my debtors and those who have trespassed against me as well as those who have mistreated me, violated me, lied on me, took advantage of me, constantly disappointed me, rejected me, and plotted against me (list them). Father I lay all this hurt at your feet, for it is your commandment that I lay aside every weight. In the Name of Jesus, I release myself from every hurt, devastating situation, disappointments, heaviness and spiritual wounds. You are a God that honors justice, and vengeance belongs to you. I lay aside every weight, in the name of Jesus.

So, Father, I choose to forgive them and as I focus on my relationship with you and I pray you touch their hearts and deal with them in a manner you see fit. I choose to forgive, let go and move forward in the Name of Jesus Christ. Regardless of how right or wrong, I choose to let go and cleave to you, my Lord, who is able to heal me and make me whole. I cannot heal myself or deliver myself. You are thy healer and you are thy deliverer. Heal and deliver me!

I release myself from every stronghold of the enemy. I will not be paralyzed by the past, anger, blame, shame, pain, and regrets any longer. This day I release and move forward into you O, Mighty God, my present help, deliverer and refuge, that I may prosper spiritually, mentally and physically.

[13] **Lead me not into temptation** (releasing process), not into flesh, not into anger, shame,

pride, stubbornness, addictions, bad habits and quick temperaments, **but deliver me from evil**, known and unknown. Deliver me from all evil (releasing process)! Deliver me from evil principalities and wicked powers, with power against the rulers of the darkness of this world and against spiritual wickedness in high places (releasing process continues).

Deliver me Father from all evil patterns of curses, sickness, diseases, afflictions and habits that have followed my family for generations (list them) down to the first. I command every curse broken in my life. Deliver me from every evil contract or agreement initiated by my maternal lineage and paternal bloodline down to the first generation, impacting my life, family and children. Let the blood of Jesus Christ cleanse and disinfect my family foundation and overturn all wicked agreements.

Deliver me from all evil, known and unknown. Deliver me from the stains of evil spoken words, mistreatment and rejection. Deliver my life, family, children's health, finances, relationships, business, ministry, future and destiny from every evil connection, in Jesus' name. For all old things have passed away and behold all things are made new for those who are in Christ Jesus. I have been adopted into the family of Jesus Christ and I am in Christ Jesus; therefore, I command my mind, body, spirit, soul and bloodline to line up with the bloodline and characteristics of Christ. I command all forms of chaos to leave my life and speak that my life comes into divine alignment with the word of God now.

Let noting hinder my breakthrough, deliverance, liberation and prosperity. According to Jeremiah 29:11 Lord, you have thought of peace for me and not of evil, to give me an expected end. Deliver me from all evil forces assigned to block, hinder, and limit my peace and prosperity. You are my deliverer; you deliver those who trust in your name. I decree and declare I shall receive the expected that you ordained for my life.

[14]For thine O, Lord is the kingdom, and the power, and the glory, forever. It is your will for me to be delivered! Deliver me O, Lord, and let my deliverance remain permanently, forever, in Jesus' Name, amen.

Un-Stuckness

Journal: notes, thoughts or ideas.

Keys to Deliverance through Prayer
Jesus' Way

Un-Stuckness

Keys to Deliverance through Prayer Jesus' Way

Un-Stuckness

Keys to Deliverance through Prayer Jesus' Way

Un-Stuckness

Keys to Deliverance through Prayer Jesus' Way

Un-Stuckness

Un-Stuckness

Chapter 6
CONCLUSION

Un-Stuckness

Following the Lord's Prayer is an excellent start to learn how to pray. I have met many people that felt that they did not know how to pray. In these encounters, I explained how effective the format of the Lord's Prayer is in addressing every area of our lives and is always recommended as being the foundation of learning how to pray, as Jesus taught the disciples.

Repenting, confessing and releasing are important keys to manifest deliverance. However, please know that repenting is also the main key that allows your prayers to be effective and favored by God. You should never start prayer without first repenting. Many don't realize that repenting is a significant step to incorporate in prayer. Often people jump straight into prayer avoiding this phase. Sometimes people also overlook giving God appreciating and thanks before making requests.

Failure to repent can block your ability to release and receive the breakthrough desired and needed. In addition, it gives Satan the advantage to block your prayers, as the accuser of the brethren.

Keys to Deliverance through Prayer Jesus' Way

He loves to complain to God day and night (when believers fall short, operate in sin, or un-forgiveness) like a spoiled child wanting his way to keep you in bondage, by some access you knowing or unknowingly gave him. He petitions to ensure that God keeps His word and laws (Revelation 12:7-12) concerning your life.

Failure to repent (and un-forgiveness) can stop God from moving on your behalf even if He wants too. When you repent, God is not restricted and His grace, mercy and the power of the blood of Jesus can freely move and fight for you. Repenting and meaning it, removes any barrier that Satan could potentially use to block your prayers from being effective and successful.

When I was in a situation where I was battling un-forgiveness, I knew how to pray but the Holy Spirit directed me to recite the Lord's Prayer every day until I was released from that stronghold and gained victory over it. Forgiving is not an easy process, nor is it an overnight process, especially not in my case. It was important to God that I forgave, and on many occasions when He told me to forgive through dreams, I told Him I could not. Then He confirmed this message through other prophets.

During prayer one day, a guest pastor came to pray over me, stating that God wanted to use me. She laid hands, started to pray and then immediately stopped and said, "I can't, you won't forgive." I was saddened that I could not receive the impartation because of un-forgiveness. I began to ask God, why I had to face such a penalty for just hurting? Still explaining why "I can't," I talked to God about everything I was feeling. We have a very open relationship and nothing goes unspoken.

The next encounter I received was at a church I was visiting. A prophet prophesized that God was going to devour the enemy and put an end to my family challenges. He ended, saying "God wants you to forgive." This inspired me to talk to God some more about my issue, emphasizing how much I love and needed Him. Further, explaining how based on my attachment and close relationship with Him, I could take a lot of things but could not endure knowing there was a separation that limits our relationship and my capacity to be used, because of this one thing that seemed impossible (I was not willing to pay this price).

When He explained how it was limiting His movement in my life, I surrendered and told Him I would try but needed His help. There was no way I could see myself being capable of letting the offense leave, but I tried and God did the rest. With my previous offense I held onto un-forgiveness for almost two years and when I decided I was going to surrender the situation to God, it took me several months (almost a year) to feel a release with evidence of an assured deliverance.

I prayed every day asking God to deliver me as I lay the offense at His feet. I reminded Him that He is a God that honors justice and that I was choosing to cast all my cares upon Him. I asked Him to provide justice on my behalf in whatever way He saw fit, as I just worshiped, prayed and surrounded myself in the safety of His peace.

In obedience, somehow the pain no longer was there, even in remembering the offense. This was when I knew the Lord had performed an operation in me and I was delivered. Not long after spiritual justice was provided and I was ecstatic with gratitude, my prayers were answered. In general, prayer is so important to embrace in life and is an opportunity that should not be taken for granted. It is one of your greatest spiritual assets. Even Jesus Christ lived a life of prayer. God does not want us to be bound, heavy and unfruitful.

Following the Lord's Prayer is how I obtained my deliverance. God wants His children to prosper while Satan wants us to be stuck, stagnated and feeling hopeless, but there is always hope when you trust in God. God loves us so much that He did not even want sin to separate us from Him. His love runs so deep and wide that no man can measure it. He made us in His image and likeness.

Keys to Deliverance through Prayer Jesus' Way

Even when Adam's disobedience "created sin and death" that separated and took us from the presence of God, Our Heavenly Father sent Jesus to redeem us, so that we will have "life" and have it more abundantly; in lieu of death.

Allowing us the opportunity to return back into God's presence the way it was initially intended before Adam sinned (John 3:16; John 14:23); this is love. That is also why there are no more condemnations for those (His Children) who are in Christ Jesus. We mean more to God than our sins, short comings or faults. Some things you just have to shake off, hold your head up, forgive yourself or someone else if required, and try again.

There is nothing we can do to stop God from loving us. Even those who are living in darkness, He loves, regardless of whether they know it or care. He loves His creations and for this reason, the sun shines on the just as well as the unjust (Matthew 5:45). We should strongly seek to live a life pleasing to God and avoid intentionally doing anything that will displease Him. He does not want us to take advantage of His love and keep using His grace as a scapegoat, to keep backsliding and falling into repeating cycles of sin.

When you pray, know that God loves you so much that He hears your prayers; believe and have faith! With this insight, you can pray sincerely in faith, knowing that He wants to answer your prayers. Be humble and patient and do not demand on timing or how and when He should move. Let God Be God and demonstrate how He moves! Pray and worship while you wait. Do it all in faith!

Ask God for the grace to have the spirit to pray and worship daily. Don't be intimidated by what some situations may look like, just speak the word of God to it and let God fight for you, rather than trying to fight for yourself; God is our shield and buckler. Let your actions demonstrate that situations have no power to manipulate your joy, control over your faith or peace of mind. Don't give the devil your power, keep what God gives you!

Keys to Deliverance through Prayer Jesus' Way

The more things look rough, repent, confess, release and let your prayers go deeper, stronger and longer. Fight the good fight of faith and once you put a situation in God's hands, leave it there and don't take it out! Jesus Christ came to destroy the works of Satan, and to give you liberation and power over all the works of Satan.

You have to enforce your rights, freedom, liberation and authority through prayer, faith and trust in God. Because of Jesus, your victory is not coming, WE ALREADY HAVE THE VICTORY!

God just wants His children to know this and operate in it, especially during various hardships and tribulations. Satan and his works have been defeated and we have all power over his works, in Jesus' Mighty Name! ALL POWER!

Un-Stuckness

Becoming A Child of God

MAKING JESUS CHRIST YOUR LORD AND SAVIOR

He was in the world, and the world was made by him, and the world knew him not. He came unto his own, and his own received him not. **But as many as received him, to them gave he power to become the sons of God, even to them that believe on his name:** *Which were born, not of blood, nor of the will of the flesh, nor of the will of man, but of God.*

JOHN 1:10-13

Keys to Deliverance through Prayer Jesus' Way

The assured way to receive deliverance is to accept the Lord Jesus Christ into your life and allow his mighty power to fight for you. You must grant God permission to intervene against the plans of the enemy orchestrated to keep you **stuck**, by bringing turmoil, struggling, hardships and disappointments.

God is more than able to uproot the negativity the enemy has planted and rebuild the foundation of your life upon the right soil, with good seeds. This allows you to become a tree planted with good roots and fruits that would flourish as a testimony for all to see.

God is able to make you become a tree planted by the river of living waters who does not fear, worry about heat or drought; but continuously bring forth fruit in its due season, whose leaves shall not wither and whatever he does shall prosper. The move of God is mighty and limitless far beyond what your eyes can see or imagine.

Making God your everything, keeping Him first and allowing Him to fight for you, rebuild, and reposition your life, will encourage the manifestation of prosperity and good health on multiple levels. The choice to receive salvation is the first step necessary for transitioning out of spiritual captivity into liberty and from darkness into light.

Repenting and accepting Jesus as your Lord, Savior and inviting Him to dwell in your heart through faith, summons the seal of the Holy Spirit of promise. And through the spirit of wisdom and revelation, your eyes may be opened to know the calling of God upon your life.

Accepting Jesus Christ and surrendering demonstrates that you no longer want to lead your own life but want Jesus to direct your path and order your steps in every way; THIS IS A LIFE CHANGING CHOICE you can make today!

> *That if thou shalt confess with thy mouth the Lord Jesus, and shalt believe in thine heart that God hath raised him from the dead, thou shalt be saved.*
> *Romans 10:9*

Keys to Deliverance through Prayer Jesus' Way

God loves you despite of your weaknesses, failures and faults, no matter how ugly or flawed and **wants to help you today** become what he ordained before the foundation of the world. All you have to do is invite Him in your heart, by using the sample prayer:

Jesus I repent of my sins and ask for your forgiveness. Today, I ask that you come into my life and become my Lord and Savior. Please wash and cleanse me from every stronghold and behavior that has created stagnation and limitations in my life. Lord I cannot make it on my own and acknowledge I need your help; today I surrender my life into your hands. May your grace help me to live a life according to the redemption and freedom Jesus Christ provided for me on the cross, this day and forever more. In Jesus Christ's Mighty Name, I pray, Amen!

_____
Your Name

_____
Date of Salvation

About the Author

Jamillah is a Mother, Licensed Minister, Author, Publisher and Inspirational Speaker. She is a youth and family advocate. *Destroy the Cage: Break Free into God's Purpose* is her first book with rave reviews and testimonies. *Un-Stuckness: Breaking Generational Chains and Strongholds Through Prayer Vol.1* is her second book in which individuals are calling POWERFUL and TRANSFORMATIONAL. May you experience your own tribute to Jamillah's writings and teachings.

Jamillah earned a Master's Degree in Criminology from Indiana University of Pennsylvania, a Bachelor of Science Degree from Pennsylvania State University in Criminal Justice with a Minor in Human Development and Family Studies, an Associate of Science Degree in Social Work: Human Services, from New Jersey's Essex County College, a Career Diploma in Child Day Care Management, and other certifications connected to this field.

She is also a member of Professional Impact NJ registry for childhood professionals, Academy of Criminal Justice Sciences and Women Speakers Association; undoubtedly a devotee for positive world

About the Author

changing initiatives. She currently works for the Department of Homeland Security as a Federal Officer, assisting with safety measures for the traveling public.

She can be requested for speaking engagements, workshops and trainings. For more information go to **www.unstuckness.org.**

If your life has been blessed by this book, please share a testimony. (In an effort to facilitate greater transformation, we ask you to please consider sharing feedback, so the next publication can be even more helpful to readers). **You can also send prayer requests.**

Please email to: **info@jamillahcupe.com,** unstuckness@gmail.com or **write to P.O. Box 22472, Newark, NJ 07101** (any comments you share would be greatly appreciated).

About the Author

Follow on:

Facebook: @ Jamillah Cupe Author Page
Instagram: @unstuckness_ministries_
Twitter: @Unstuckness

Available for:

Trainings
Workshop
Speaking

Send invitation request to:

info@jamillahcupe.com and
unstuckness@gmail.com

Thank You!
May God Bless You Above and Beyond Your Imagination!

www.ingramcontent.com/pod-product-compliance
Lightning Source LLC
Chambersburg PA
CBHW060833050426
42453CB00008B/674